Preparing
and Evaluating
Liturgy

Bernadette Gasslein

NOVALIS
THE LITURGICAL PRESS

Design: Eye-to-Eye Design, Toronto

Layout: Suzanne Latourelle

Illustrations: Eugene Kral

Series Editor: Bernadette Gasslein

© 1997, Novalis, Saint Paul University, Ottawa, Ontario, Canada

Business Office: Novalis, 49 Front Street East, 2nd floor, Toronto, Ontario M5E 1B3

Published in the United States of America by The Liturgical Press, Box 7500, Collegeville, MN 56321-7500

Novalis: ISBN 2 89088 800 2

The Liturgical Press: ISBN 0-8146-2444-8
    A Liturgical Press Book
    Library of Congress data available on request.

Printed in Canada.

Gasslein, Bernadette
    Preparing and evaluating liturgy

(Preparing for liturgy)

Includes bibliographical references.

ISBN 2-89088-800-2

1. Catholic Church–Liturgy. I. Title. II. Series.

BX1970.G38 1997   246L02 C97-900986-3

Contents

Introduction

In my workshops on preparing and evaluating liturgy, the first question I usually ask is: "What happens when people from your parish get together to prepare liturgy?"

Often, participants talk about the conflicts that seem unresolvable, the frustrations that the group experiences. They talk about spinning their wheels endlessly, for instance, in trying to decide what kind of flowers to use for decorating the church for a particular season—and where the flowers should go. Others talk about the drop-out rate on their committee because the same issues recur, and people just get fed up talking about them. Or they speak of situations where, no matter what the liturgy committee does, the priest does it his way, anyhow. Sometimes they sum it up as boredom: "We do schedules."

Rarely do they speak of their task in terms of a ministry. That's for others—lectors, musicians, hospitality ministers, catechists. Even rarer still seems to be an experience of formation for the task they are undertaking. Many indicate that they have not read such basic documents as the *Constitution on the Liturgy (CSL)*, or the *General Instruction on the Roman Missal (GIRM)*. Often my workshop is the first they have attended that deals specifically with their ministry.

Preparing: A Big Job

Liturgical preparation is a big job. In fact, the scope of the series to which this book belongs indicates just how complex this task is. People who are preparing liturgy need to be able to work with a number of basic components: the liturgical year, music, the environment, the lectionary. They need to deal with specific groups, such as children or youth, and do so in various settings, such as school or parish. They need to examine different tasks, such as presiding, serving and preparing the eucharistic table.

They need to be aware of various rites of the church, such as Christian initiation, and morning and evening prayer, and how a parish can celebrate these. In short, these people must be able to address skillfully a whole series of issues and questions as they go about the task of preparation. This book sketches in general what that task is, pinpoints the basic skills for and attitudes towards this ministry of preparation, and why it is so important. Furthermore, it links the process of preparation to its sister process, evaluation.

Evaluation: Not Necessarily Terrifying!

The word evaluation raises other terrors. Most people have little or no experience of this process as related to liturgy, even though it is probably a regular aspect of their working lives. Often what they do remember about liturgy and evaluation is a situation in which, under the guise of evaluation, someone was attacked personally and left wounded. Others recall efforts at evaluation that bogged down in a vicious circle of opposing factions, where one group liked a particular liturgical experience and the other didn't—and no one seemed able to break the impasse. Given these experiences, they remark: "People don't want to be criticized. It's already hard enough to get people to commit to ministries. If you start talking about evaluating them, they're all going to quit. Then what will we do?" Others ask how something as sacred as liturgy can be evaluated.

Evaluation worth the name doesn't leave people feeling wounded, attacked or diminished. Like preparation, it sets both the church's vision of liturgy and our experience of this action of praise and thanksgiving at the centre of its reflection. Evaluation both affirms the work that the ministers of preparation have done, and urges them to tune their activity more closely to both the church's self-understanding of liturgy and the needs of the local community gathered for worship. It recognizes the sacred work that God's people do in liturgy, and strives to enable them to undertake this as well as possible.

This book does not detail all the issues you must address to prepare every aspect of liturgy; the rest of the books in this series do that. Rather it is designed to help you understand the processes of preparation and evaluation themselves, and begin to use them effectively in your parish.

Planning or Preparing?

In his ground-breaking book, *Preparing for Liturgy: A Theology and Spirituality*, revised edition (Chicago: Liturgy Training Publications, 1997), Austin Fleming introduced into our thinking the vital distinction between planning and preparing (pages 31-41). Local communities receive the readings, prayers, rites, etc. that have been carefully planned, and prepare them so that the community can celebrate them. The following comparison summarizes the differences between preparing and planning:

In planning	In preparing
• we create the terms of the encounter with God	• we prepare for an encounter with God, the mystery who calls us together
• we tinker and toy with the form of the ritual so that it fits our sense of how it should be	• we receive the gift of the shape and form of our ritual
• we can avoid the "tough stuff" of the gospel or the ritual, thus escaping its power to draw us into the process of ongoing conversion	• we accept that the readings and ritual, though they may not be new, may challenge us in unexpected ways, for the Spirit of God moves in our celebrations

The process of preparing and evaluating liturgy, understood properly, does not have to be fraught with difficulties. In fact, preparing and evaluating can draw your community more deeply into the celebration of the mystery of the living God. That's what this book is about.

In Summary

1. Liturgical preparation is a complex task.

2. Evaluation both affirms the work of the community, and challenges it to live its celebrations more fully.

3. Preparing and evaluating draws us more deeply into the celebration of the mystery of God.

Discussion Questions

1. Describe your parish experience of liturgical preparation. What is life-giving in it? What would you like to change?

2. What has been your experience with evaluation?

CHAPTER 1

Standards for Preparation and Evaluation

As we begin to explore the process of preparation and evaluation, it is crucial for us to know exactly what we are preparing and evaluating, and from where we derive the standards for both preparation and evaluation.

We Prepare the Assembly

In the recent past, most preparation has focused on particular ministers—musicians, lectors, communion ministers, servers—and the technical aspects of their ministries. Some people have thought that the more ministers are involved in the celebration, the more the "full, conscious, active participation" of the people is promoted. The unspoken sub-text to this was that if you weren't involved in a particular ministry, you weren't really as involved in the liturgy as you should be.

The past few years have seen the gradual emergence of a new consciousness of the assembly as the celebrant of the liturgy, "through, with and in Christ." With this new awareness, new questions have emerged, along with a new focus for particular ministries. How do we encourage the assembly's participation? How do we enable the assembly to assume its "right" and "obligation" to praise God? How do the particular ministries relate to the assembly's fundamental responsibility to worship?

We've also asked other basic questions: What is the assembly? How do we help people to recognize that they "are the people of God, purchased by Christ's blood, gathered together by the Spirit, nourished by his word … a people called to offer

God the prayers of the entire human family, a people giving thanks in Christ for the mystery of salvation by offering his sacrifice … a people growing together into unity by sharing in Christ's body and blood … holy by their origin, but becoming ever more holy by conscious, active and fruitful participation in the mystery of the eucharist" (*GIRM*, 5).

Another booklet in this series focuses on *Preparing the Assembly to Celebrate*, and offers lots of practical tips on how to help people come to this self- and God-awareness. For our purposes here, it suffices to recognize that the focus of our preparation will be the assembly. If we speak of particular liturgical ministries, it will be to ponder how they serve the assembly's fruitful participation in the liturgy.

If Liturgy Is All This, Then …

Vatican II's *Constitution on the Sacred Liturgy* offers a number of important descriptions of liturgy that are important for the ministry of preparation.

> … the outstanding means *whereby the faithful may express in their lives and manifest to others the mystery of Christ and the real nature of the true Church (2)*
>
> … *an exercise of the priestly office of Christ … (7)*
>
> … *a foretaste of that heavenly liturgy celebrated in the holy city of Jerusalem … (7)*
>
> … *a sacred action* surpassing all others; no other action of the Church can equal its effectiveness *by the same title and to the same degree … (7)*
>
> … the summit *toward which the activity of the Church is directed; at the same time it is the* fount from which all *the Church's power flows … (10)*
>
> … *the source for achieving in the* most effective way possible *human sanctification and God's glorification, the end to which all the Church's other activities are directed … (10)*

... the primary *and* indispensable *source from which the faithful are to derive the true Christian spirit ... (14)*

The *GIRM* describes liturgy as:

... the high point *of the work that in Christ, his Son, we offer to the Father ... (I, 1)*

... the action of the whole Church ... (I, 5).

Note the highlighted words! These insights challenge us to ponder how we treat this activity. One participant in a workshop I was giving remarked, "I didn't know liturgy was so important for the church—I just thought it was liturgists making a big deal of it." Her observation accurately reflects the attitudes of many people at various levels of responsibility in the church. It raises the important question of the kinds of resources—time, money and talent—we invest in liturgy, both at the local and the diocesan levels. If liturgy is "the outstanding means whereby the faithful may express in their lives and manifest to others the mystery of Christ and the real nature of the true church," then what kind of investment do we, as a community, make in it? How do we prepare this activity?

The Effects of Liturgy

Now, let's examine these descriptions of the effects of liturgy. According to the *CSL*, it:

... daily builds up those who are within into a holy temple of the Lord, into a dwelling place for God in the Spirit ...

... strengthens their power to preach Christ ...

... shows forth the church to those who are outside as a sign lifted up among the nations (2)

... moves the faithful to be one in holiness ...

... prays that they may hold fast in their lives to what they have grasped by faith ...

... draws the faithful into the compelling love of Christ and sets them on fire ... (10).

Recently, I participated in a focus group in my own parish, which was chosen to be studied as "an effective parish" (for the results of this study, see Donald Posterski, *Future Faith: Leading*

Edge Churches for the 21st Century [Winfield, B.C.: Woodlake Books, 1997]). Gathered around the table were men and women who had been part of the community for two to forty-two years. What struck me as I, a member for a scant two years, listened to my sisters and brothers in this community was how important the parish's liturgical life was for their outreach to the wider community. Again and again, people spoke of how the liturgy enables them to reach out to the poor, to the broken, to the shut-ins. These men and women were really set on fire. The effects of our liturgy were truly manifest in the community's life. Liturgy well celebrated has a profound effect on people's spirituality—and not just according to liturgists!

The Goal of Preparation

What sets people on fire? The *Constitution on the Sacred Liturgy* provides the goal that those who prepare liturgy need to keep before them if they want to provide this kind of spark:

> *"In the restoration and promotion of the sacred liturgy, the full, conscious and active participation of all the people is the aim to be considered before all else, for it is the primary and indispensable source from which the faithful are to derive the true Christian spirit"* (CSL, 14).

The document makes two important connections in the same article, First, it indicates that this "full, conscious and active participation in liturgical celebrations … is demanded by the very nature of liturgy." Then it indicates that we have a right and obligation to this full, conscious and active participation because of our baptism (14). Our baptism calls us to praise and glorify God, not because of any law, but because we have been made part of the body of Christ; we do what the body of Christ does, which is to offer God glory and praise.

"The very nature of liturgy" is an important phrase. Understanding the nature of liturgy is indispensable for those who will prepare it. In the next chapter, we will examine it.

In Summary

1. Standards for preparing and evaluating derive from the church's vision of liturgy.

2. Liturgy is the action or work of the whole assembly, not just the ministers or the liturgy committee.

3. Liturgy is supposed to be effective: it is vital to parish life and outreach.

Discussion Questions

1. Examine the descriptions of liturgy found on page 10. How do they challenge your current way of preparing liturgy?

2. Does the liturgy in your community foster a sense of prayer and service? If you asked people what gives them the strength to live their Christian lives, would the Sunday liturgy figure in their response?

CHAPTER 2

The Nature of Liturgy

The nature of the liturgy provides the framework in which the ministry of preparation unfolds. There are two fundamental aspects to this nature: theological and ritual.

The Theological Nature of Liturgy

We can identify five fundamental characteristics of the theological nature of liturgy.

- Liturgy is *trinitarian:* we praise God the Father, through the Son, in the Spirit who enables us to pray. The whole Trinity is involved in our action.

- Liturgy is *christological:* in the church's liturgy, Christ prays, and the church prays in Christ. Everything about this celebration proclaims his paschal mystery, and invites us to participate in his passage through self-emptying living and death to new life in the power of the Spirit.

- Liturgy is *ecclesiological:* it is an action of the church, the body of Christ. It identifies us as a people of praise; because praise is part of our nature, the activity of praising God flows from our very being. We participate in this activity "by right and by obligation": not to do so would be to deny who we are in the depths of our being. Such an approach casts a very different light on the nature of the Sunday obligation, which, in this context, is constituted more by our identity than by an external law.

- Liturgy is *eschatological:* in it, we participate, in Christ, in the ongoing heavenly liturgy, worshipping with the angels and saints. It enables us to see this fullness of life that is promised in the future, not just in our imaginations, but in the relationships, the actions, the sounds and silences, the tastes and flavours of this feast of life. As a foretaste of the heavenly liturgy, it invites us to glimpse what we can now only see dimly.

- Liturgy is *incarnational:* it always passes through our bodiliness, affirming that God speaks and acts through human flesh. Therefore, the privileged mode of activity in our celebrations is ritual, that unique configuration of symbol, gesture, metaphor, music, time, action and structure through which God acts in our lives, and we participate in God's life.

The Ritual Nature of Liturgy

All of this remains abstract if we fail to recognize that liturgy's theological nature can only be accessed by the other face of its nature, ritual. This face of liturgy has three aspects:

- *Ritual:* the repeated actions, patterns, forms, gestures and structures in which we engage when we celebrate. Rituals are behaviours repeated in a particular order; we engage in them with others, and in a meaningful way. Their sequence and structure itself has meaning—take for example, the liturgical year. Repetition frees us to enter into the ritual. Because ritual belongs to groups of people, it's important not to change it often, because the more frequent the change, the more difficult will be the community's ability to enter into the ritual.

- *Symbol:* the word symbol comes from two Greek words, *sun* and *ballein*, which mean "to throw together." Symbols are created realities—bread, wine, water, oil, people—that establish, evoke and embody a variety of relationships and invite us to participate in those relationships with our minds, our feelings, our bodies and our imaginations. Because they invite and evoke, they elicit many meanings. Anyone who has experienced, for example, a raging storm at sea, the power of a hurricane's rain, and the cool delight of a summer swim knows that water can both give life and deal death; we know also that fire warms, illumines, transforms and destroys; human beings love and betray. Only if the symbols of our liturgies are full enough so that people do not have to intellectualize their meanings but can experience them directly through their senses of taste, touch, smell, sight and hearing can these symbols elicit a range and depth of meanings in the members of the assembly.

- *Words*: Many kinds of words—similes, images and metaphors—mark our celebrations. The scriptures employ many different literary forms, and, in poetry, song, saga and parable, tell many different stories of human beings in relationship with their God. The language of the prayers continues the process of remembering, recalling in vivid images God's wonderful works before presenting our needs to God. Listen carefully to the words of the various prayers: this is not the kind of language you would find in the "how-to" manual for your computer. Carefully crafted, these words, as the word "metaphor" implies, are designed to take us elsewhere: in this case, into the mystery of God.

Through Ritual via Theology into Mystery

The basic challenge for those preparing for liturgy is to hold together these two aspects—theological and ritual—of the nature of liturgy. Ignore the theological aspects, and you will end up doing theatre: honourable, but not your task, or you will create empty ritual. Ignore the ritual aspects of liturgy, and you will have a theological construct, but no liturgical experience. Again, an honorable thing in itself, but not your task. As Gil Ostdiek remarks in *Catechesis for Liturgy* (Washington: Pastoral Press, 1986), "Liturgy is a matter of *experienced meaning*, not explanations" (12, emphasis added).

Most of your ministry in preparing liturgy will deal with the ritual face of liturgy. This task is demanding because two factors have contributed to our tendency to ignore this face. First, while we are good at theologizing about ritual, we tend to be hesitant about taking seriously the incarnational aspect of liturgy that demands that we enter into the ritual experience. We should celebrate, not primarily with our heads, but with our hearts and bodies. Yet, many people would prefer to just think about liturgy instead of feeling it: getting wet or oily, being touched, or eating and drinking. To enter into this experience, we must relinquish the control our heads like to have. Where will it lead us? What will happen to us in this encounter with the living God?

The other factor in this reluctance is that ritual, like an art form, imposes limits that result from its form. Recently we have tended to reject these limits as inhibiting creativity. In fact, quite the opposite is true. Just as the interplay between the limits established by any art form and the drive to break beyond those limits constitutes a major element of creativity, so in liturgy the limits that ritual imposes create an experience that we cannot entirely control, and thus can draw us more deeply into the mystery which the theological nature of liturgy articulates.

Your community's way of celebrating, will, over the years, fashion in people, without them even being aware of it, answers to such basic questions as "Who is God?", "What does it mean to be human?", "What/who is church?" This characteristic is one of liturgy's most subtle effects: even without noticing it, the ritual activity in which people engage provides them with a theological vision of the world. If well done, it will speak the incarnation and paschal mystery more loudly and clearly than any theological discourse. If poorly done, it will fail in this basic mode of strengthening people's faith. Failure to take seriously the two aspects of the nature of liturgy will ultimately impoverish the faith of the people of your community.

In Summary

1. Liturgy has theological and ritual elements that must work together. We access the theological via the ritual.

2. Ritual that is familiar and known by the assembly allows the assembly to be the agent of its worship.

3. Ritual ties our experience to the present, creates a new vision of God at work among us, and shapes our behaviour as disciples of Jesus.

Discussion Questions

1. If you had only your own parish's liturgical celebrations as an experience of faith, how would you answer the following:

   • Who is God?

   • What is a human being all about?

   • What/who is church?

2. What one word describes your experience of faith as communicated in your parish's celebration of liturgy?

CHAPTER 3

Preparation and Evaluation: Definitions

Now that we have laid out some of the basics, it's time to examine more closely the meaning of preparing and evaluating liturgy. I owe thanks to the participants in my course at the Summer Institute in Pastoral Liturgy at Saint Paul University, Ottawa, Canada, who for the past three summers have contributed their ideas and critiques to the definitions I use throughout this book.

Preparation: A Definition

> *The process by which a particular celebrating community interprets and enfleshes the rites (gets the words and rubrics off paper into action, proclamation, gesture, ritual, song) so that the assembly can celebrate the paschal mystery through full, conscious and active participation in the Church's liturgy.*
>
> *Participants in this process listen to the community's [e]valuation of liturgical celebrations to build on identified strengths and remove or transform hindrances to participation.*

Let's look at each element of the definition in more detail.

1. A process

The *Collins English Dictionary* defines process as "a series of actions that produce a change or development." Included in the series of actions that liturgical preparation entails are meeting, studying, reflecting, imagining, discussing, choosing, deciding and implementing.

You will work out this process on three time lines: long-term, seasonal, and immediate or weekly.

Long-term preparation begins with the liturgical year, one of our chief ritual resources, and its shape. Identify the high point of the liturgical year: the Triduum. It only makes sense that if this is the culmination of the liturgical year and the heart of our celebrating, you will invest much time and energy in preparing it. Don't forget that it is a single feast that stretches over four calendar days: it must be prepared as a single feast, not a series of isolated celebrations. But remember that you are not preparing it in isolation: its gestures and symbols and, to a certain extent, even its music, are also included in our celebrations throughout the rest of the year.

The other festive seasons are Easter, Christmas, and their preparation times, Lent and Advent. Study the readings for the seasons as a group (for more on this approach, see *Preparing the Table of the Word* in this series). Prepare Lent-Easter and Advent-Christmas together so you can attend to the links between the seasons as well as their distinctive aspects.

Once you proceed in this manner, you address many of the details that affect your weekly celebrations: the environment and the music will probably change little from Sunday to Sunday. Choreograph the rite so that it unfolds in much the same way each Sunday so that its familiarity will allow people to enter into it more deeply. Discourage individual presiders from changing it each week and, if necessary, adjust, rather than change, the rite from Sunday to Sunday.

2. A particular celebrating community interprets and enfleshes the rites

We have ritual books: *Lectionary, Sacramentary*, various ritual books, *Sunday Celebration of the Word and Hours*. They contain most of the words and the rubrics for our celebrations. The *GIRM* offers both commentary on and interpretation of the rites. Liturgical preparation advocates for the full implementation of the various options included in such documents as the *GIRM*, and subsequent documents.

If only one person were acting in this celebration, and if preparation only involved reading over words, then it would probably be left to that person. But all of us who gather to celebrate are engaged in this action. Rubrics are no longer for the priest alone, as the *Constitution on the Sacred Liturgy* (31) and a quick perusal of our liturgical books indicate. To involve people in this sacred action, consider a particular celebrating community: What is the age of the people in the community—are there lots of children or mainly retired people? Are the demographics of the community changing? How many people are there? Look at the space in which the community is celebrating: what shape is it? what size? Is a space that was build for 1,000 now being used by 250? Has it been well renovated? What is its sound? What about the quality of light? Can people move around in this space? What is the ethnic background of the community? How are various cultures integrated into the community? Are there animosities? Are differences viewed as challenges or as gifts? What resources are available to this community? Have musicians and other artists been invited to share their gifts with the community? Are print and other resources made available, either locally or from the diocese, for people to continue their learning on liturgical topics? What is the liturgical history of this community—has it embraced liturgical renewal and enjoyed ongoing formation or has there been a general unwillingness to explore these topics?

How you answer these questions will—and should—colour the choices and the interpretation of the rites you make when you "get the text off the page." They yield a profile of your [changing] community that will help you determine what, at any given moment in your community's history, "full, conscious and active participation" might look like. This same profile will also provide you with information you need to plot a course of pastoral action that will enhance your community's ability to celebrate more fully, more consciously, and more actively each year.

Enfleshing the rites means precisely that: taking words and rubrics (you may want to think of them as "stage directions") and enabling your people, with their bodies, young or old, to make them their own. Be careful not to stereotype the range of people's responses according to age or gender; for example, young people can enter into silence and old people can dance! (For a more detailed list of the various actions we do in liturgy, see page 25.)

3. Celebrate the paschal mystery

Have you ever tried to determine the theme for the liturgy you're preparing during a liturgy committee meeting? Can you recall the wrangling and debate around its exact formulation?

Relax. You never have to go through that agony again, for when you prepare liturgy, you know that liturgy has one theme, and one theme only: the paschal mystery, expressed in many different ways in the liturgy, and embodied in many different ways in our lives.

This mystery is the story of our paschal God who is always pouring Godself out into our history, first as one who heard the people's cry of anguish, and rescued them "with outstretched arm and mighty hand," who pitched the nomad's tent among us and walked before them as a pillar of fire. In Jesus, this God takes on our flesh with everything that limits us: the Creator becomes creature. We see the utter otherness of God, in human flesh, in one like us. We look on him, as we look on each other, and live.

This mystery announces God's unending faithfulness, for the God who takes on flesh in Jesus does not abandon him to death, but walks with him into this final and most devastating of human experiences, holding on to him in love and compassion. God never lets go of Jesus, and so raises him from death as the first-born of all creation, and brings him, in his wounded humanity, into the glory that is the depths of the heart of God. God gives him the name of Lord, and joins all humanity for ever to this great movement. Now the Spirit of their love that is stronger than death is poured out on all the world, so that all who know us may hear this good news and come to know the God of Jesus Christ.

This mystery is so unfathomable that it needs a lifetime of telling and retelling the story. Thus we can learn to see it, recognize it, name it, hear it, taste it, smell it and touch it with our own hands (1 John 1). It is the mystery we call paschal: the first and ultimate story of God and of humanity in God.

From this mystery the assembly takes its identity. No matter the brokenness, the sinfulness, the tragedy, no matter the delight, the creativity, the triumph, our God does not abandon us, but walks with us through the joy and the devastation of our lives to a place where Life does triumph over death. As you look around your community, you probably know people who are experiencing one or the other aspect of this dying and rising very keenly: the couple who has lost a child, the couple on the next street who is celebrating the birth of a child; the newly-weds in the first blush of their life together, the divorcing couple who both weep for the love they could not cultivate. The list is long; you can probably add to it from your own life. The paschal mystery marks the whole of our lives; it sums up Jesus' experience of God: God is faithful, no matter what. Not even death could separate Jesus from God. Christ offers praise and thanks for this faithfulness; we who live now in him do the same.

The stories, symbols and gestures of our celebration all tell this story in their own ways. In fact, keeping this dynamic in mind as we prepare our celebrations will offer new insight into all aspects of our celebration. This can happen only if we are unafraid to embrace the dying in our own and each other's lives, so that we might celebrate Christ's triumph in our daily reality.

4. Full, conscious and active participation

While these three descriptors are connected, it might help to look at them separately.

- Full participation. Lay people are full participants in the liturgical action, not second-class citizens. In *The Assembly Celebrates*, James Challancin has pointed out how the hierarchical ordering of the liturgy described in the *CSL* actually includes lay people. Most people would be surprised to realize this. He reminds us that the word "hierarchy" is derived from the Greek word for "holy." All God's holy people celebrate the eucharist, carrying out those actions that belong to them.

- Conscious participation. Hopefully you're awake when you come to celebrate the sacred mysteries, because not only will you need to be awake, but also to be conscious of what you're doing. You're able to recognize that you're giving praise, or listening, or reflecting, and you deliberately choose to do so.

We also need to recognize another aspect of this participation: *un*conscious participation. Earlier, I noted that symbol appeals to the whole person, including the imagination. Only through symbol can we engage the deepest and most unreachable aspects of our person: the depths of our unconscious. Sometimes when we can't detect much happening on the surface, we discover later what has been growing and changing in the depths of people's lives beyond their conscious awareness.

- Active participation. Active participation goes hand-in-hand with having a place in the celebration. Our job is not to be spectators at the priest's celebration, but to assume our rightful role, for "all the church's a stage and all the men, women and children players." What do we do?

Often, people are hard pressed to identify more than two or three activities that we do in liturgy. But consider the following list that indicates the variety of actions in which we are engaged. The column on the left lists the action; the one on the right comments on the action as it might be described in the liturgical context:

1. come in — assemble
2. sit — for a ritual, not for watching TV
3. stand — together, ready to participate
4. sing — not a solo, but as a group: the Body of Christ
5. speak — at specific times for the ritual's purpose, singly and together: to ask forgiveness, to praise, petition, acclaim, proclaim.
6. respond — with established words
7. listen — listen to the word
8. see — observe; our eyes are delighted or disappointed
9. pray — in silence, aloud; pray with/for
10. smell — incense; candles
11. taste — the rich taste of bread; the rich taste of good wine
12. eat — eat a ritual meal
13. imagine — focus our imaginations
14. walk — process
15. move — ritually, in gesture or in time to music
16. read — proclaim
17. serve — serve the holy bread and cup
18. carry — carry a book or gifts in procession
19. shake hands — offer peace
20. embrace — offer peace
21. drink — share the cup of the Lord's very self
22. break bread — remember and commune in the Lord's gesture of self-giving
23. welcome — welcome to the Lord's house
24. set the table — set the table of the Lord
25. be silent — pray in silence at the appropriate moment

Does your community do all these actions consciously? Have you paid attention to these actions and how they are executed? If not, they provide a fruitful forum for the investment of your energy.

5. The church's liturgy

Those who prepare liturgy must recognize that they minister to the church's liturgy; it is bigger than their own parochial vision. Those preparing must be prepared to explore the church's vision thoroughly, and to correct or expand current practices so that parish practice reflects the ecclesial vision, not their own. This means knowing and understanding the various options of the rites, and how to implement them.

6. Participants in this process

Who prepares liturgy? At some level, everyone who participates. The particular ministers certainly need to prepare for their activity. They should undertake this preparation with the assembly's participation in mind. And certainly the presider should prepare—both individually and with the group whose special ministry is preparation.

Whether we should call this group a "committee" is open for discussion: it depends on the style of working together that the word "committee" evokes for you. This group of people gathers to make ready the place, the people and the things of the celebration; it has both a long-term and immediate perspective. It is inclusive, but not necessarily representative. Pastoral leaders need to discern who can work together—not because they agree with each other on every issue, but because they have the skills to do it. Who will commit to the process? Who values the community's liturgical life? Who will view this as a ministry, that is, a service to the community, not a power trip? Have we drawn from people who normally attend celebrations at different times each weekend? Have we included older people and younger people? People from different backgrounds? Remember: not everybody can or should be on the committee!

This working group should include members of the assembly who have no particular liturgical ministry, as well as musicians, presiders, homilists, hospitality ministers, sacristans, lectors, communion ministers, and servers. You do not necessarily have to select the leaders of these groups, as long as those participating can accurately communicate discussion and decisions to other ministers.

To engage in liturgical preparation, people need a willingness to learn from and to mine the often-dry, but still rich, resources of the official documents. Preparation processes will otherwise flounder, since they lack a solid foundation on which to build and by which to measure decisions.

People will also have to learn about how ritual behaviour works; this is more difficult, because in addition to print resources, it takes a keen sense of observation of good ritual over a period of time, along with some kind of guided reflection, to recognize ritual patterns and how they work. Students in my classes who reflect on and discuss the liturgical action daily for two weeks have reported at the beginning of the second week that they are starting to see things differently, and catch things they would have missed earlier.

Liturgical preparation needs people who operate out of an *ecclesial spirituality*. This means that all who work at this ministry must recognize that they are part of a larger reality, the church, the body of Christ. They must be ready to embrace the vision of the larger community and relinquish pet ideas and practices when they fail to respect or live up to the eccesial vision of our liturgical celebrations.

Liturgical preparation also requires people who have developed an *incarnational spirituality*: all who work at this ministry must recognize that God's fullest revelation continues in and through Christ's body, the church. An incarnational spirituality recognizes that God's salvation is embodied and inculturated today in the rituals, symbols and gestures of the liturgy. Those with artistic skills and vision make an important contribution to developing this spirituality, as do those who have a keenly developed sense of movement and space.

If members of your working group do not have at least a nascent sense of these two spiritualities, they will have a hard time collaborating in the process of preparation.

Other practical group skills include flexibility, non-combativeness, reliability and a positive outlook on life. It will be important for pastoral leaders to develop some sense of how much time people will be asked to commit to this process, too. Some, such as musicians, may give much more than others, but, in our over-committed society, unrealistic expectations of time commitments will only hurt the process.

7. Listening to the community

How do you know what people have experienced in a given celebration or season? Listening to and reflecting with members of the working group and, more importantly, with people who didn't belong to that working group, will provide you with insight. There is always a danger, if the group engages in this process only with its own members, that they mistake their intentions in preparing with the actual experience of the celebration. It's easy to get caught up in, "But what we wanted to do was ..." Once you've celebrated the liturgy, what you wanted to do doesn't really matter; what actually happened—what people experienced—is what the process of evaluation must deal with.

[E]Valuation: A Definition

Once again, let's examine each aspect of the definition:

> *The process of focused [mystagogical] reflection that enables a community to deepen its consciousness of its call to praise God and intercede for the world. It builds up the body of Christ by reflecting on liturgical celebrations, affirming what promotes the "full, conscious, active participation" of the assembly in Christ's work of praise and intercession, and identifying hindrances to this participation.*

1. Focused or mystagogical reflection

The effectiveness of this process rests in the questions we ask about our experience. I will say more about this later; for now, what is significant is the mystagogical aspect of this approach. As a form of mystagogical reflection, the process of evaluation helps us explore the sense of the mystery we have celebrated. It deepens our awareness of how God works in the liturgy and thus elicits our thirst for an even fuller experience of the mystery.

2. Deepened consciousness of our call to praise God and intercede for the world

Evaluation must explicitly focus on whether we are doing what the liturgy intends us to do. For this reason, it is not enough to simply ask, "Did we pray?" The question is too broad, and subject to far too much individual interpretation, for each of us has an operative, but often unarticulated, definition of prayer. Such a question risks bogging the group down in wrangling over a definition!

The basic question to ask is: "What in this celebration enabled me to praise God?" I'll explore this question further in Chapter 5.

3. It builds up the body of Christ ...

Evaluation that tears people down, leaves them with hurt feelings, totally discouraged in their ministry or wanting to excommunicate other parishioners does not build up the body of Christ. After all, liturgy is a human action, and human beings make mistakes and have bad days.

Evaluation often reveals the need for formation. If people indicate that the incompetence of lectors, musicians, presiders or homilists is a hindrance to praise, then the parish needs to look seriously at providing formation for these people or, in some cases, to help them discern a ministry more fitted to their individual gifts. These two options build up, rather than destroy.

4. Affirming what promotes the participation of the assembly, and identifying hindrances to this participation ...

A contemporary understanding of evaluation also includes the sense of *valuation*—hence the "[E]Valuation" that you noticed earlier in this chapter: strengths, accomplishment and gifts are identified and affirmed. You cannot ignore this essential aspect of the process without disempowering everyone in your working group.

Nor can you ignore hindrances to participation. Here again, being focused is the key. If you ask, "What hindered your praise?", this specific question directs those engaged in this process to be very focused. They may even discover that something they didn't *like* didn't keep them from praising God!

In Summary

1. Clear definitions of preparation and evaluation facilitate both processes.

2. Full, conscious and active participation of the whole assembly is the goal of preparation.

3. Focusing on praise in the process of evaluation enables participants to build on strengths in celebration, and identify and remove hindrances.

Discussion Questions

1. Using the definitions presented in this chapter, identify the strengths and limitations of your preparation and evaluation processes. What can you build on? What needs to change?

2. How would you describe yourselves as a "particular celebrating community"?

3. What does it mean to you to operate out of an ecclesial spirituality? What pet ideas might you have to relinquish?

CHAPTER 4

Basic Principles for Preparation

As you undertake the ministry of preparation, let these principles guide you.

1. Repetition is the Basis of All Ritual.

Ritual is made up of patterned, repeated words and actions. The resulting familiarity enables the assembly to enter into these words and gestures easily. This familiarity is an absolute pre-requisite for "full, conscious and active participation" of the assembly in the liturgy. People will find themselves, not wondering what they're supposed to do next, but becoming free to pray together in familiar words and common gestures that lead them into the mystery of the living God.

This has several practical consequences for the ministry of preparation. It means that you do not, in fact, should not, re-invent the wheel from week to week or even from year to year when preparing the liturgical seasons. Give much thought to every new gesture, movement or piece of music that you introduce into the celebration. Rarely introduce something that will be used only once. Even a celebration such as the Easter Triduum employs gestures and patterns of celebration that are part of our liturgical vocabulary throughout the entire year. (For more information on this, see the chart "Glory Days" in *Preparing the Liturgical Year 1*, in this series.)

Sometimes people will accuse you of not doing your work properly if something isn't new every week. Resist with all your might the temptation to evaluate your preparation based on the criterion of the amount of newness in the celebration.

2. The Contour of the Rite Is Central.

Each rite has a shape, and within our rites are smaller ritual units whose shapes result from high and lower points. Learn to articulate the relationships among these different elements of the liturgy of the word or liturgy of the eucharist, so they don't just follow one on the other, all at the same speed and with the same intensity (or lack thereof). These differences make the liturgy engaging, and create a dynamic between these smaller liturgical units.

The communion rite provides the climax of the eucharistic liturgy. Would observers (and participants!) know by the way it is celebrated that this is the climax of the eucharistic celebration? Its procession is one of the four of the liturgy. Does your parish process to share in the holy food and drink of the Lord's table? Or do they amble along or, as someone once called it, have a communion stampede? Is this an intentional movement that embodies the sense of purpose and unity that the GIRM ascribes to the communion rite (56i)? What kind of movement does the music chosen support? Only if you know the shape of the rites can you work out their various elements in such a way that the form of the rite will embody its purpose.

3. Move from the Big Picture to the Smallest Component.

Start with the broadest categories, and end with the most particular, because the latter are situated in the context of the former.

One of the best examples of this process, which you may wish to view with your preparation group, is the Liturgy Training Publication video, *Say Amen to What You Are.* It offers viewers the opportunity to examine how one parish has developed its communion rite over a five-year period. It provides an excellent example of a well-prepared rite within the whole celebration.

Clearly, those who prepared this rite understand, have studied and reflected on the GIRM, 56. Using this understanding as a basis for their preparation, they have moved forward. I will just highlight a couple of aspects of their implementation.

The video shows all the processions of that community's liturgy, which clearly links the procession of the gifts and the communion procession. Leaders have helped their community develop the role of the procession in the liturgy as a whole and a sense of the communion procession in particular.

Persons in the assembly present themselves to the communion minister, who cups the communicant's hand with one hand and presents the body of Christ with the other. This sense of intimacy, heightened by touch, is made possible by the presence of a second minister who holds the plate of blessed bread. The joy on the faces of both minister and communicant is tangible; nothing about this exchange is hurried. All are joined by song as well as by their sharing in the body and blood of the Lord.

One choice depicted in the film gives rise to much discussion. The decision that communion ministers would share in holy communion last reflects the sense that servants serve others first; the other position, which the Canadian Church encourages, is that communion ministers give what they have received. Such a choice cannot be made without measured discussion about the merits and drawbacks of each position.

Still, one thing is clear: Knowing the big picture has enabled them to enflesh this rite in their community through careful attention to the smallest details. It will do the same for you.

4. Respect the Structures of Rites.

You don't start with communion and end with the liturgy of the word. While this may seem an extreme example, it illustrates the kind of ritual nonsense that results when we don't respect the structure of the rites. Just as the language we speak follows certain conventions that give it intelligibility, so the language of ritual has its own conventions that make it intelligible to participants. The structure of the rites takes us in certain directions: from beginning to end, from listening to responding, from the table of the word to the table of the eucharist.

When preparing, don't fiddle around with this structure. Know the available options and work within them.

5. You Can "Set" the Intensity of the Ritual.

Everyone knows instinctively that there's a difference between an ordinary supper and a party. One factor that contributes to the difference is called *intensity*.

A "quick bite" reheated in the microwave while you change your clothes to dash to the next meeting probably is the lowest level of ritual intensity that a meal could exhibit. A wedding banquet illustrates a much higher level of ritual intensity that happens when the best food and drink that money can buy are served on well-appointed tables to guests who sport their best clothes, eat by candlelight, offer toasts, and collect slices of ritual cake to tuck under their pillows. What we might traditionally term "atmosphere" (created by the environment—candles, flowers, tablecloths, music, etc., and the common purpose that brings the group together), ritual dress, the food, and the ritual order in which the celebration unfolds, all intensify the experience of sharing a meal together, and make it a memorable occasion.

You can turn up the intensity of your parish celebration in a similar way. Music is a basic way of intensifying the ritual. In ordinary time, you may use a simple accompaniment to the acclamations of the eucharistic prayer. For the Easter season, you many add more instruments, or even raise a fairly low tune a half or whole tone. You might add harmonies or descants. Or, during Lent, you may add quite a different kind of intensity by singing those same acclamations unaccompanied.

Touch also intensifies ritual. For instance, in infant baptism, the presider, and parents and godparents may make a barely discernible cross on the infant's forehead or one that all can see and "feel." During the exorcism prayer from the scrutinies of the RCIA, the presider can stretch out hands in the general direction of the elect, or lay hands on each, praying silently for a few moments.

Symbols can be clear, rich and sensual, or minimal. Monitor this kind of involvement, because it is easy to appeal to only one or two senses (many of our celebrations focus on hearing and/or seeing to the exclusion of the other three senses). Such limited appeal decreases involvement in the liturgy. Those who participate in communion should be able to taste the goodness of the Lord and drink in the richness of God. The psalmist who invites us to "Taste and see" (Ps. 34) makes an interesting connection when he suggests that the experience of one sense (taste) will lead to a new insight of another sense (sight). This illustrates the connection between the theological and ritual nature of liturgy: theologically, we say that God is good. In this instance, liturgy wants us to experience this, through taste, and come to this insight, not to start with the understanding, and consider the symbol a nice, if somewhat unnecessary, illustration. To produce this kind of insight, both senses must be sufficiently stimulated. Minimal symbols cannot provide this.

Movement also intensifies ritual. Given the architectural limitations of many of our churches, we need to remember that raising arms, assuming the *orans* position for prayer, walking in procession or inviting the whole assembly to participate in a few simple dance steps are all invitations to deeper involvement in the community's praise.

You may want to include some aspects of intensified ritual (such as communion under both kinds, which corresponds to both the Lord's command and the climactic nature of the communion rite) at all of your celebrations, while reserving others for special seasons or feasts.

6. Pacing and Rhythm Are Critical to Good Celebration.

Have you ever left a celebration breathless because every aspect of it was rushed, or sleepy because it dragged? Each of the parts of the liturgy has its own purpose and character, and needs its own time.

Silence is an important aspect of pacing the ritual. But silence is part of the ritual itself, so do not extend silences unduly, add them where they don't belong or ignore them all together. A common experience of imbalance is a twenty-minute homily in a forty-five minute celebration. Such a practice suggests that the other parts of the celebration are unimportant, and probably manifests that the homilist has either not prepared properly, or does not understand the homily's purpose. (For more on this topic, see *Preparing to Preach* in this series.)

Rhythm moves a piece of music along. The steady pulse that causes us to tap our toes draws us into the movement of the music. Over and around that, the melody weaves its magic as its notes sometimes land on the beats, sometimes between them, sometimes on strong beats, at others, on weak ones. Just as the notes in a piece of music have different values and thereby lend interest to the piece, so the parts of the liturgy have different values. Within the liturgy of the eucharist, the preparation of the gifts and table is a preparation rite; it is not the eucharistic prayer. Musically and ritually, then, it must not overshadow the central prayer of the celebration. The introductory rites must not be longer than the eucharistic prayer. If everything takes the same length of time, the celebration will become as ponderous as speech in which each syllable receives the same accent, or music in which every note has the same value.

7. Dialogue Is an Essential Aspect of All Liturgy.

The assembly celebrates liturgy; in this celebration dialogue has a privileged place. There is, certainly, the dialogue that leads us into the great eucharistic prayer, and there is also dialogue that unfolds more subtly: the "Let us pray" that leads to silence which leads to the collect in which the presider voices the community's prayer. The liturgy of the word ritualizes the dialogue between God and humanity. God speaks; we respond in song, word, prayer and faith. The presider invites the assembly to voice its praise in the acclamations of the eucharistic prayer.

Preparation must take into account this fundamental dialogue to ensure that no one voice dominates, monopolizes or is excluded from the celebration.

8. Music Is an Integral Aspect of All Liturgy.

Liturgy is essentially musical. The music you choose must match the action the community is doing. For instance, eucharist is essentially the body of Christ's action of praise and thanksgiving. Do the texts of the hymns enhance and support the liturgical action? Does the gathering hymn unite the assembly in a common action or dissipate its energy? Is the gospel acclamation a laconic nod to the ritual or an energetic herald of the good news we are about to hear? Do the eucharistic acclamations enhance the unity of the eucharistic prayer, and its sense of praise and joy?

The question of music in celebration is so central to good liturgical preparation that it has its own book in this series, *Preparing Music for Celebration.*

9. Symbols Express and Shape Faith. They Always Need Preparation.

The liturgical action turns around several primary symbols: the assembly, the liturgical year, the word, the table, the bread and cup, water and fire. Often those preparing the liturgy ignore these fundamental aspects of the liturgy to focus on peripherals such as banners and themes. Always focus on the primary symbols. This makes your job much easier. See the bibliography for other books in the series that will help you explore these central symbols.

10. KISS: Keep It Simple, Sweetie!

"Noble simplicity" marks all good liturgy (*CSL*, 34). If your celebrations are becoming more and more complex, stop and rethink what you're doing. The first nine principles mentioned here should make your life much simpler. You can prepare whole seasons at a time; you don't have to change—in fact, you shouldn't change—your ritual patterns and actions each week. You can focus on the essentials, and, as you do that, you'll discover that many of your dilemmas resolve.

In Summary

There are ten basic principles of preparation:

1. *Repetition* is the basis of all ritual.
2. Attend to the *season*, the *feast*, the *text*.
3. The *contour* of the rite is central. Form embodies purpose.
4. *Music* is an integral aspect of all liturgy.
5. *Symbols* express and shape faith. They always need preparation.
6. *Structures* of rites must be respected.
7. *Rhythm* results from the interplay of structures.
8. *Dialogue* is an essential aspect of all liturgy.
9. *Balance* is created by intelligent choices.
10. KISS: Keep it simple, sweetie! (Noble simplicity marks all good liturgy.)

Discussion Questions

1. Using the liturgy of the word or the liturgy of the eucharist, map out its high and low points, and the relationships among the different elements.

2. How can you develop the processions in your parish?

3. Identify and describe the different levels of intensity in your parish celebrations. What do they reveal?

4. How are symbols dealt with in your community's celebration?

CHAPTER 5

Working at Evaluation

Four things are important in the process of evaluation: who does it—and when, the questions you ask, the answers you receive, and what you do with that information.

Who Does It—and When

Those who were involved in the preparation process should be involved in the process of evaluation. The responses they hear will be invaluable to them for the community's ongoing ministry of preparation. But the group should also be enlarged to include at least a few people who were not part of the preparation process, lest the group mistake its plans for the actual experience that people had.

You may want to invite wider consultation by publishing the basic questions in your church bulletin with a brief explanation to the parish about why you're asking these questions. People may not offer you written answers, but they will be less startled if members of the preparation group ask them to share their responses to these questions.

You should evaluate weekly, seasonally and yearly. (Weekly evaluation is normally quite brief.) Pose these questions soon after the liturgy (or season) has finished. If a group cannot gather each week, get into the habit of jotting down your answers to these reflective questions before the meeting. Time is a factor because ritual experiences tend to transform themselves in our memories as they do their work. While this may not hinder our religious experience, it can contaminate the evaluation process.

The Questions

As I mentioned in Chapter 3, the basic questions to ask in the evalution process are "What in this celebration *enabled* me to praise God?" and "What in this celebration *hindered* my praise?" These questions are important for several reasons.

First, to know whether we are doing what the liturgy is designed to do, we must design the questions to address that reality. Therefore these questions focus on the basic goal of liturgy: praising God. By doing so, they provide people with a lens through which they can read their experience, and help them overcome the often-prevalent sense in our culture that liturgy's goal is to make us feel good. This in turn increases the respondents' consciousness of praise as an essential aspect of celebration, a consciousness that they re-invest in both the process of preparation and their own liturgical prayer.

Second, it invites an "I" response: respondents must assume responsibility for their own reactions, thoughts and feelings. In the group dynamic, this is absolutely fundamental: it reduces blaming and polarization, and moves the reflection beyond personal taste. It offers all the participants time to hear what others have to say. Some of the most interesting discussions often turn around different people's reactions to the same event or symbol. Don't fear these varied reactions; symbols are powerful because they can evoke different responses.

Third, these questions hold together the two faces of the nature of liturgy—theological and ritual—described in chapter 3. To answer them, people must reflect on the ritual and its relationship to the theological.

Fourth, these questions set a tone for the process of evaluation: no one is out to get someone else; no group is targeted for praise or criticism. By drawing us back to the ritual details, they avoid, as much as possible, issues of personality.

Finally, these questions don't ask if someone *liked* the celebration. They ask if the ritual was effective in helping them praise. Once again, this takes us beyond personal preferences or styles into the ritual action.

What enabled me to praise God?
What hindered my praise?

When a group is beginning the process of reflection, I usually work with the first question for at least two sessions before adding the second question. In answering this question, the group begins to acquire the skills to articulate the experience of the celebration.

Take, for example, the question of hospitality. Suppose a liturgy preparation group decides that they are going to at least shake hands with, and preferably kiss, everyone who comes through the church doors as a gesture of hospitality. Everyone thinks this is a great idea. The weekend arrives, and the hospitality committee is in place.

Come the evening for evaluation, one of the persons reports having asked a friend in the parish the two basic questions. She was a bit stunned by the response: "I was so put off by that guy trying to kiss me at the door that I almost turned around and left. Praise? I fumed my way through mass!"

Others report similar responses; still others note that some people were delighted by the warmth with which they were greeted, and noted that they had felt really wanted there, something that had made them want to praise God even more.

These responses have garnered some very important information for the group to work with preparation. Should they abandon hospitality? Of course not! Should they adjust what they had prepared? Yes! They might recognize that they had focused on only one, quite effusive, style of hospitality that would disturb many people. They must not abandon the principle of hospitality, but broaden the range of ways in which they embody it so that it does not have the opposite effect to what they had desired. Without this significant feedback, they would have not been able to correct a potentially serious problem. So, along with eliciting people's feedback, you will also want to elicit their suggestions for adjusting or modifying something that is proving to be a hindrance, or invite them to suggest how you might continue to build on positives.

Once you have gained a bit of skill in dealing with these questions, you can move on to other questions designed to address other facets of the liturgical experience. To do this, people must be growing in their familiarity with how the different aspects of the ritual embody the theological nature of liturgy. (Knowing the liturgy documents will open up many avenues of reflection for you.) To facilitate this process initially, the text in roman type provides some aspects of the celebration to examine.

Was I respected as a member of the body of Christ in this celebration? What aspects of the celebration give rise to my answer? You might consider those aspects that explicitly demand the assembly's response: The various dialogues, the silences after "Let us pray." Did the people have time to answer at a dignified pace? Was there silence during which they could collect their own prayers?

Was the dignity of the assembly revealed in this celebration? What aspects of the ritual served this? How could our dignity have been better revealed? Respect: in words and gestures? Were any excluded? Put down? Did the homily help the people realize that God is at work in them, in their world?

Did the assembly, with its diversity and diverse ministries, reveal the fundamental unity of the body of Christ? How? Were all engaged in common movement? Common song?

Did the various ministries enable me to praise and thank God? What was most helpful? least? Could I hear the reading? Did I understand it? Did it catch me up in the story? Did I sense that I was actually eating at the Lord's table? Did I experience genuine hospitality? Was the assembly encouraged to sing, or was all the music given over to the choir?

Did this celebration help me see how the paschal mystery marks my life? our lives? How? Why not? Are people welcome in our parish, even if their lives aren't perfect? Does the homily help us develop our sense of God's working in our midst, even in situations that at first seem hopeless or devastating?

Do you experience the eucharistic prayer as the heart and centre of liturgy? What contributes to or detracts from this? Are people standing around, bored? Is it proclaimed or delivered? Are the acclamations sung?

How do people in your parish experience the communion rite? Was there a sense of communion? What contributed to this? What would enhance it?

Does your parish community prepare the eucharistic prayer? Why or why not? How does it do this? Is this the priest's prayer or the assembly's? Does the preparation committee have access to the texts of the prayers?

What are the connections between the homily and the eucharistic prayer? Does the homily leave people eager to praise God or asking for merciful release from listening?

When evaluating the seasons, you might proceed by taking the description of the season from the *General Norms for the Liturgical Year and the Calendar*. Use it to formulate a question such as this one for the season of Lent:

Did we get in touch with the sense of renewal of baptism during Lent? How was the penitential aspect of Lent linked with this? What aspects of the celebrations helped with this?

An especially important question to ask when evaluating the yearly experience turns around the centrality of the Triduum. It's easy to say it was the high point of the year, but you need to check more deeply to verify what, in fact, was the high point.

The Answers—and What to Do with Them

First, respect the answers. This is a kind of faith-sharing process; people are making themselves vulnerable. Remember that and honour it.

Second, like the preparation, the answers fall into several categories: immediate, seasonal and long-range. Some, as in the scenario described above, will impel you to almost immediate action. Others you will file carefully until you begin your preparation for the next time that liturgical season cycles around.

And, when you evaluate your whole year's experience, you will need to be able to refer to both the responses, and what people might have proposed to adjust something or remove a hindrance.

What happens if there are lots of hindrances to praise, and few helps, especially if these focus on, for example, the function of one person, such as the presider?

Honesty and a sense of the good of the community are crucial for all concerned. Honesty concerns your own reaction. It does not cover personal conclusions about other persons. The good of the community insists that you share your reactions in a respectful manner, and be ready to listen to responses. Given the common nature of our liturgical action, you are probably not alone. Change cannot happen without such honesty, but it can only happen constructively if all involved are willing to work together for a common goal, and distinguish personal taste from what the church sets forth as its understanding of the nature and function of liturgy.

In Summary

1. Involve people in the evaluation process.

2. Evaluate weekly, seasonally and yearly.

3. The questions asked in the process of evaluation should explore both the overall liturgical experience and its details.

Discussion Questions

1. Select one of the questions in this chapter, and work with it.

Simple Gestures, Profound Impact

We prepare our celebrations because we believe that what we celebrate, the paschal mystery, is our source of life. We prepare real interactions that help the assembly experience the life to which we are called: the life of hospitality to all, the life of proclaiming the word; the life of prayer for the world; the life of praise and thanksgiving; the life of service to all; a life which remembers that the simplest of gestures, the breaking and sharing of bread and cup, carries the most profound impact.

The actions we undertake in liturgy are but an icon of the actions we are called to in our ordinary, everyday life. Not all are lectors; all must proclaim the word from day to day; not all are eucharistic ministers; all are called daily to serve brothers and sisters, to do justice, to feed the hungry, to comfort the sorrowing. All are called to praise and thanksgiving, at all times and places. If we see, over and over again in these celebrations what we are called to be and do in all of our life, our hearts, minds, bodies and imaginations are gradually formed by the workings of ritual, by the movement of symbol until a piece of bread broken and shared becomes, not second nature, but first; until visiting the imprisoned becomes a way of life for us who have been released from all our prisons by the one Lord and Saviour.

Having been enabled by the Spirit and by the ministry of preparation to experience the love of God in our assembly, and to respond with praise and thanks, we go out in the peace of Christ. Having experienced ourselves as the body of Christ in the assembly, we know how to discern the body of Christ in the world: I was hungry ... thirsty ... a stranger ... naked ... sick... imprisoned, and we know how to respond: take, eat ... take, drink ... we touch, we listen, we proclaim, we embrace, we embody the love of God for all we meet. Our ministry is not just for the sake of the assembly, but for the sake of the world hungry for the wholeness of God's reign.

Why Does This Feel So Familiar?

Here in our celebration, says the *Constitution on the Sacred Liturgy*, we have a foretaste of the heavenly liturgy to which all are invited. Let the imagination of your heart consider this: when the people of your community die and, entering the Kingdom of the God who is Alpha and Omega, find themselves led to the banquet table with the tax collectors and prostitutes, with the prophets and the martyrs, with the patriarchs and the matriarchs, with their parents, their children, their lovers, their friends, their enemies, will they pause a moment and say, "Why does this feel so familiar?"

Will they be able to answer, "Of course! I remember this. So it was with our celebrations in my parish. Yes! There, too, were ministers who welcomed me … there, too, was a rich banquet— oh, the stories, yes, the stories of God's compassion. And yes, yes, this bread that gives life—yes, I've broken this bread before, and I have tasted the rich wine of the kingdom before, though I now know the best has been saved for the last! Yes, this song is familiar, for you taught me to sing God's praises in your assembly—and I will praise him still."

That will be our ultimate evaluation. If, because of their experience in our assemblies, the people in our communities can answer in this way, we will have prepared our celebrations well.

Catechesis: "the whole of the efforts within the church to make disciples, to help people to believe that Jesus is the Son of God, so that believing they might have life in his name, and to educate and instruct them in this life and thus build up the body of Christ" (*Catechesi tradendi*, 1).

Mystagogy: in its most general meaning, a form of reflection based on the liturgical, ritual experience. By savouring and exploring the meaning of the words, rituals, symbols and gestures, it helps participants enter into them more deeply so that, when they come to celebrate these mysteries again, they will be able to do so with greater depth, joy and engagement.

Spirituality: the dynamic process by which human beings give form to their lives by discovering, creating and living out ultimate meaning. Turning around a central core, it expresses itself in connection with ourselves, our history and our God.

BIBLIOGRAPHY

Recommended Reading

Ritual Books

The Sacramentary, The Lectionary and their introductions are essential reading for those preparing and evaluating liturgy.

Books and Articles

Preparing for Liturgy Series (Ottawa: Novalis; Collegeville: The Liturgical Press, 1997):

Aldi-Wanner, Kim. *Preparing the Assembly to Celebrate*.
Bick, Margaret. *Preparing to Celebrate in Schools*.
Bonneau, Normand. *Preparing the Table of the Word*.
Britz, Andrew, and Maier, Zita. *Preparing Sunday without the Eucharist*.
Corcoran, Bill. *Preparing the Rites of Initiation*.
Eddy, Corbin. *Preparing the Liturgical Year 1: Sunday and The Paschal Triduum; Preparing the Liturgical Year 2: Lent-Easter and Advent-Christmas*.
Glendinning, Barry. *Preparing the Eucharistic Table*.
　Preparing to Preside.
　Preparing to Preach.

Hibbard, John. *Preparing to Serve at the Table.*
McNorgan, David. *Preparing the Environment for Worship.*
Reid, Heather. *Preparing Music for Celebration.*
Richards, James. *Preparing Morning and Evening Prayer.*
Sweet, Marilyn. *Preparing to Celebrate with Youth.*
Whitty, Gerard, Mercer, Jeanette, and Wells, Elaine. *Preparing to Celebrate with Children.*

Challancin, James. *The Assembly Celebrates. Gathering the Community for Worship.* Mahwah, N.J.: Paulist Press, 1989.

Fleming, Austin. *Preparing for Liturgy: A Theology and Spirituality* (revised edition). Chicago: Liturgy Training Publications, 1997.

Gasslein, Bernadette. "Evaluating the Parish's Liturgical Celebrations" in *National Bulletin on Liturgy,* Vol. 30, Number 150, Fall, 1997.

Hausling, Angelus A., ed., Linda Maloney, Trans. *The Meaning of the Liturgy.* Collegeville, MN: The Liturgical Press, 1994.

Hoffman, Elizabeth. *The Liturgy Documents.* A Parish Resource. Third Edition. Chicago: Liturgy Training Publications, 1991.

Kavanagh, Aidan. *Elements of Rite. A Handbook of Liturgical Style.* New York: Pueblo, 1982; Collegeville, MN: The Liturgical Press, 1990.

Metzger, Marcel, Madeleine Beaumont, Trans. *History of the Liturgy: The Major Changes.* Collegeville, MN: The Liturgical Press, 1997.

Ostdiek, Gil. *Catechesis for Liturgy.* Washington, D.C.: The Pastoral Press, 1986.

Searle, Mark. *Liturgy Made Simple.* Collegeville, MN: The Liturgical Press, 1981.

Periodicals

Celebrate! Ottawa: Novalis. Published six times yearly; provides solid, up-to-date resources on a wide range of pastoral liturgical topics, and background for working with the Sunday readings.

National Bulletin on Liturgy. Ottawa: CCCB. Published by the National Liturgical Office of the Canadian Conference of Catholic Bishops. Solid, scholarly articles on various liturgical issues.